A Spirit of One

By

William Moss

ISBN: 0-7596-9522-9 (E-book)
ISBN: 0-7596-9523-7 (Paperback)
ISBN: 0-7596-9524-5 (Dustjacket)

This book is printed on acid free paper.

1stBooks – rev. 12/03/02

Line Of Heredity

Date of Heredity

Birth Name

Oat Oat

Late 1700s Caddo Chief, a signer of the 1835 Land Cessions Treaty with the United States of America. A descendant of thousands of Hereditary Chiefs.

1859 *Oat Enoch Hoag*

Son of Oat. Last of the Caddo (Hasinai) Chiefs before the American government reorganization of Indian Tribes.

1871 *Oat Thomas Wooster (Worcester)*

Son of Oat. Mr. Blue, half brother of Enoch Hoag. (Hasinai) Spiritual Leader. Thomas Wooster married Roxie (which means Chip Falling from the Moon). They had a son named Whitemoon and Roxie died during childbirth. Whitemoon was raised by Roxie's mother, Choah, a Spiritual Leader, who was Kadohadacho, Hainai, and Hasinai.

1893 *Oat Michael Martin*

Whitemoon, grandson of Oat. Silvermoon was his artist name. He was one-half Hasnai, one-fourth Hainai, and one-fourth Kadohadacho.

1964 *Oat William Moss*

Grandson of Michael Martin, Last of the Oat.

(The Caddo Chiefs traced descent in the father's line - all other Caddo traced their families on their mother's side.)

Contents

Part Two

The Seventeen Books of Wisdom

Chapter

Introduction

It is believed by the Caddo that they have inhabited the continent of North America since the beginning of time. Caddo history has no record of the crossing of this race and culture from Asia, and teaches that the race's first existence was in America.

Before the fifteenth century, A.D., and some time after, the Caddoan-speaking peoples resided in and ruled the territory from what is now the Gulf, and Gulf Coast, northward to the middle of Canada, bounded on the west by Colorado and east by Iowa. Some of the lands were held in common with other tribes, who later became the dominant inhabitants.

Kadohadacho means Real Chiefs. The Caddo were a peaceful, agrarian society whose principal crops were squash, corn, beans, and tobacco. The Caddo did hunt buffalo and turkey. Caddo also fished rivers, lakes and in the Gulf ocean. Life was orderly and was directed by a Council of Chieftains made up of both spiritual and tribal leaders. The Supreme Chief was multi-talented and attained both spiritual and tribal leadership within the Council of Chieftains.

The Caddoan Linguistic Family consisted of communities. Each community or Band had several hundred or thousands of individuals who were ruled over by their tribal and spiritual leaders. Each had a separate name and a Caddoan language dialect. The largest and most dominant if the Caddo community Bands were the Hasinai. Prehistory may have general differences, however, American documented history describes the Hasinai as composed of the following Bands/Tribes: Hasinai, Nasoni, Haanai, Nacono, Neches, Nacogdoche, Nawidish, and Anadarko. The next largest prehistoric and historic Band was the Kadohadacho, or Caddo proper. This Band/Tribe community was, at the time of recorded history, composed of the Kadohadacho, Quachita, Doustioni, Nantosoho and the upper and lower Natchitoches. The third group of Bands/Tribes were the Haish, Yowani, Kichai, Nadaco, and Nasoni. Other Bands/Tribes were the Haish, Yowani, Kichai, Nadaco, and Nasoni. Other Bands were independent tribes such as the Hais, Adai, and Yatasi.

The Caddo predominantly inhabited the geographical area which is the State of Eastern of Oklahoma, Western Arkansas, Northwestern Louisiana, Northeastern Texas, and Southwestern Missouri within what is now the United States of America. These communities of Bands/Tribes made up the Caddo Confederacy. Although dispersed over a wide geographical area, each Band was very similar in belief systems, clothing, custom, and speech.

The dominant band of the Caddo was Hasinai, which at the time of recorded American history made its primary home in what is now Louisiana and East Texas. In this dominant ruling band the supreme hierarchy was passed on through marital heirship, at birth receiving the ruling family hereditary ascribed position. The blood-line of the family of Chief Oat, prehistorically and historically were trained from known conception to be the best of men. The Oat Supreme Chief and Oat Chiefs and their families traveled to each of the other Bands/Tribes on a regular basis to make decisions of law, domestic and foreign policy, commerce, and the economy, and to participate in spiritual and cultural events.

Today, in the 1900's, many Caddo live in the State of Oklahoma, and in the surrounding areas of Binger, Loekeba, Ft. Cobb and Anadarko. Although the Caddo were one of the most dominant and populous tribes in the south before the 18th century, there are now only about three thousand, on the Caddo Tribal rolls and many are of mixed blood. The Caddo fell more often to death due to epidemics which came to America with the Europeans than to wars.

The prehistoric, historic, and spiritual information contained in this book was gathered in the traditional method of teaching of the Caddo, which is both verbal and non-verbal communication, passed from one generation to the next continuously since prehistoric times. Written, oral, visual, and genetic knowledge was obtained from one of the last full-blooded Caddo, Michael Martin, direct descendant of the Chief Oat family. Michael Martin, an artist by trade, was also a tribal leader and a Caddo historian who worked with prominent scholars regarding Caddo history. He was born in approximately 1893 and died in 1969. He lived with and was raised by his great- grandmother, Choah, who was a recognized tribal and spiritual leader.

The contents of this book were assembled and recorded by William Moss, grandson of Michael Martin, and last of the Oat. The book is divided into chapters which are presented in two parts. The five chapters in Part One contain the Caddo teachings about the Universe, Life, and Man. Part Two presents the Rules for Living designed as Books of Wisdom. All contents of this book have been personally synthesized in thought by the author, William Moss, and written for the first time in English.

Part One

The Universe, Life and Man

William Moss

Chapter I

Foundations of Life

God

The foundation of all life and existence is creation by the Creator, God. God is the focal point of all existence within the universe. Without God nothing would exist and everything is owned by Him. God is the basis of life-spiritually and physically. God is, and is all that is.

The Caddo word for God is *Ah-ah-ha'-yo*, which means: God; Father in Heaven; Creator of the Universe.

Breakdown of creation:

- God creates space

- Space into universe

- Universe into earth

- Earth living life

- Plants and animals

- Humans above all

- Human to God

God creates the universe for his pleasure: Earth, plant life, animals, and humans. God is loving and wants all creation to exist within happiness so that He might look upon His creation and be pleased.

The universe is in the absolute will of God. He controls it at His will. The plant life of earth is set and bound to continual cyclical existence by Him. Animals live a cyclical revolving life of essentially the same experience, though varying from species to species. They are content and in harmony. God created man with an eternal spirit, soul, and a will to choose left or right, bad or good.

God is pleased with the soulless life of the universe: plants, rocks, dirt, water, and animals. Yet man does not live up to God's standards of life. Man wrongs his neighbor, commits sins and defiles God's own creation - Man. Man is displeasing to God. Man's duty to his Creator is to be pleasing to Him. Without the Creator man would not exist. Though man should only try to be pleasing at his own sincere will.

Positive and Negative Forces

Within the universe there are different forces that effect the different elements:

Spiritual Properties:

- God and Devil

- Good and Evil

- Heaven and Hell

Electrical Properties:

- Positive and Negative

- Right and Wrong

- Love and Hate

Physical Properties:

- Light and Dark

- Solid and Liquid

- Rock and Dirt

Complementary Opposites:

- North and South

- West and East

- Right and Left

- Vertical and Horizontal

- Height and Depth

There is a path to follow in life for good eternal existence. There is a path to bad eternal existence.

One must always strive to stay on the good path of life. If he strays from it, he must get back on it, lest he continues down the bad path of life and is eternally damned.

An honest acceptance that there are differing forces in life must be accepted; basically, that there are good and bad forces within the universe. An honest acceptance of this within one's mind is essential. Without it one immediately denies the truth and lies to his own mind, making way for further misunderstanding of life.

Spirits

God created good angels that by their will turned bad; choosing bad with their leader in opposition to God. God created a place in darkness and depth for the devils to exist in Hell.

Good angels seek to please and serve God.

Bad angels seek to displease God.

God's greatest creation unto Himself are angels, then man. God seeks worship and companionship from angels and man. Man has a will and can be influenced by either good forces or bad. It is man's will to choose. Bad angels seek to displease and hate man and God, continuously tormenting them. Good angels love God and seek to guide man, look over him, and love him.

Both forces exist and wave either positive or negative force. Yet it is for each man to decide his path by his will.

Space and Time

God created all that exists, nothing else exists before Him or after Him. God is the beginning and the end. Yet, in actual fact, there never was a beginning nor will there ever be an end in time. God is always.

Time is measured by light and dark in an earth day: one-half light and one-half dark. The time frame is one. The next day is the same - only a different period of time. There are no separate times, all time is one and moving forth. Time is not to be wasted, it can never be regained, it is one of the single most significant dimensions in life.

Space is everywhere and its existence is never ending. From the solid floor of earth up, there is space. The space in space never ends. There is no wall to its existence.

Space and time are one, there is no beginning or end.

Eternal Existence

Eternal is forever. Man's eternal existence begins at conception. His physical life continues forth in a linear path of age until his physical death. His spirit and soul lives on eternally, never ending in time.

On earth and in eternity, man may seek happiness. The only way to achieve happiness is to live a life of pure action in thought, word, and deed. With a pure soul after physical death on earth, the soul, if pure, moves into Heaven at God's will.

The soul of man lives in eternal happiness for millions upon millions of years - infinitely.

The impure soul goes to Hell and exists in unhappiness infinitely.

The pure soul on earth might be tempted morally or materially, just as the impure soul was yet choose to act in a righteous and pure manner. His pure soul was judged to live in Heaven eternally. The impure soul was judged to live in Hell eternally.

Although the impure soul might have lived on earth in greater material happiness or thought in the midst of immoral happiness, this action might have lasted for only an earth age of maybe one hundred years. Now he lives in Hell for millions upon millions of years in eternal unhappiness. The pure soul might have encountered and denied the same temptations for a hundred years until his death. Now he lives in eternal happiness for millions upon millions of years, infinitely.

The pure soul is not only righteous but logical in time.

This created universe is only a fragment of the imagination of God. In time, time on earth is like one pebble out of billions on a beach of sand.

The Will

It is only by God's gracious will that all the universe exists. The earth, wind and fire are controlled by God. God controls creation and the life cycle until the time He wills to discontinue this earth. Everything that exists is in the controlled will of God: earth, animals, and especially man.

In the creation of man, God inset a free will choice to allow man to choose between right and wrong, left or right. Man is at his free will in action, God only watches over man and sustains his existence. God does not force man to love or hate Him. He leaves it up to the will of man to choose.

To sin by one's will should aggravate man's physical body, to sickness, and his mind to ache that he has displeased his Creator in action. Man must force himself to certain goals; a mindset of his forceful will to avoid sin, to attain commitments of purity and eternal existence.

Man and Woman

God is a spirit, intangible, though taking form, He is man.

Man is the superior counterpart to woman. Man is in the form and image of God. Man takes on the mannerisms of his Creator.

- God is God.

- God is man.

- Man is man.

- Woman is woman.

God's Spirit sustains His creations.

Chapter II

The Mind of Man

Mind

The mind is the foremost instrument of thought and action in man's life. Every thought that is thought within a man's past, present, or future is from his mind. The brain is the physical central point of intangible thoughts of the mind.

The spiritual and physical body of man moves in directions of what his mind tells him: right or wrong, left or right. Thoughts are intangible, and the body is physical. Thoughts transfer the physical body into action in the present, as in the past and will in the future. Actions are recorded in the memory of the mind.

To keep a pure mind, one must think pure thoughts, and act pure in physical action.

Conscience

At conception and in birth man is innately given a discernment between good and evil; the conscience of man is to instruct his life. One knows right from wrong without ever being told by another man. His conscience tells him continuously what thoughts to perform with action.

To keep a pure conscience, one must always act the righteous way. He must follow his conscience, as a personal law, and choose right. If one chooses the wrong path, and continues on that path, his conscience will deplete. His mind, becoming impure, will no longer be able to decipher right from wrong. Choosing wrong, he will see wrong as right, and right as wrong. His mind becomes negative and impure, leading toward a wrong path of life.

Therefore, to keep a pure conscience one must always act right. If one does wrong, confess and be done with it, then continue again down the right path of life with a good conscience.

A pure conscience is a main ingredient to a pure and happy life.

Good and Bad Action

Within the mind, thoughts become actions. If good action is to prevail over a bad environment, one must keep his environment pure: persons of association, things and places. If a decision is to be made of persons of good associations, there is only a choice of good action to be chosen. If a choice is between good action and wrong action, a person exposed to a bad person's influence, he might become as his association, and choose wrong. Then, negative while in that environment, more than once, he falls into a bad environment and can eventually become impure.

The same is true with material objects of environment and places. To sustain purity within one's being, one must keep himself away from impure persons, material things and environmental places.

If man is only in a good environment, then only good can be chosen. If in a good and bad environment, then either good or bad can be chosen. If only in a bad environment, then only bad can be chosen. Therefore, a pure environment is most safe to the mind, soul, and body.

Good and bad action are always a choice, yet the good choice is always the right choice.

Action, Not Words

It is better to act and do what one professes to do, than to speak of it only in words.

Words are inanimate and only present an expression of thought. Action is done, and is remembered by the one acting as well as those that he has acted upon.

Do what one will do for good, but do not speak of what one desires to do and does not. Do only what you think in action and experience and no words will be needed.

Honesty

An honest mind makes a content body and soul.

It is honest:

- That God is first and Creator.

- God is a spirit and man.

- Man is superior to woman.

- Man needs woman and woman need man.

- That good and bad spirits exist in the universe.

- That all choices are either right or wrong.

- There is light and dark.

- There is a Heaven and Hell for everyone's eternal existence.

It is honest:

- That if man and woman love each other and make love normally and morally, it is good.

- That if man and woman love each other and make love abnormally and immorally, it is bad.

- That if man and woman do not love each other and make love normally and morally, it is wrong.

- That if man and woman do not love each other and make love abnormally and immorally, it is bad.

It is honest:

- That in life there is a way to do things and there is a way not to do things.

- There is a good path to follow in life and a bad path.

- That bad spirits will try to influence one to do wrong, and good spirits will influence one to do right.

- That good is superior to evil.

- That positive force overwhelms negative.

- That light is greater than dark.

It is honest:

- That to survive, man needs utmost food, a dimension of love, and a sense of sexuality; secondary is shelter and clothing.

Being honest to the Creator that His creation is good, is honest. Being honest in his life about forces and choices in life is only a realization of life itself. One not realizing right or wrong, left or right, height and depth, only lies to his mind, body, and soul. Therefore, it is real to be honest and accept reality as it is. Be pure not impure, choose positive not negative, choose right not wrong. Choose the honest path of eternal life toward Heaven, not the dishonest path of eternal life toward Hell.

It is good to be honest of reality. Honest to be righteous to one's mind, body, and soul; and righteous to one's own Creator.

In honesty man will achieve parallels and views toward the thought of God. Honesty, in itself, is the core of all life.

Chapter III

The Body of Man

Genes

The body of man, when born into physical existence, is an overlapping process of already established hereditary genes. Hereditary genes are the main inlay of the physical body, creating a mind, a body, a place for the soul of a being. Therefore, to make strong beings, both a man and a woman should be physically strong in body, have a strong will of mind and a pure moral soul.

Parts of the Body

Physical Body

A strong physical body is imperative to the benefit of one individual. Man can walk, run, push or pull with a strong physical body. Nothing within his bounds of environmental existence should bind him. Man's physical body should be as strong as possible, within the limitations of himself. Man, in fact, should be confident about his own body and know its strengths and weaknesses.

Man's physical body holds the intangible parts of his being: mind, spirit, and soul. With a strong physical body, man can make all parts of his being stronger. Therefore, to be complete, all parts of a man's being must remain strong and intact.

Mind

Man's thoughts are to be in a radius of thought to past, present, and future at every moment, making the physical action of his body progressive toward eternal existence. The mind should think pure thoughts of beauty and love, reasonable thoughts of daily decision, and rational thoughts of love and hate, thereby producing in every thought a considerate, logical solution to each task of the mind.

The mind should avoid bad experience. Once an experience is over, it is recorded in the memory to be forever remembered. The mind should desire to experience good opportunity to record at the present, because the present becomes the past, now remembered in the memory as abundant good experiences.

If bad experiences are numerable in the memory of man, then that man, at his own task, should make good experiences innumerable in his mind. Therefore, the mind should keep a strong positive outlook, not negative.

The mind directly and indirectly controls the body, the spirit and soul. The mind is the focal point of an individual and to reach eternal existence, one must keep a pure and strong mind.

Spirit

The will of man is to relate to the will of God. It is man asking for God to indwell in spirit within his body, making him a spirit of good. Man is never to ask for any evil to possess him or be about him. Man is a subject of his Creator, logically created for good, not bad. Man's innate spirit desires to be good. Therefore, he must keep on a path of positive action, building a strong spirit, to be one with God.

Soul

The soul of man exists forever after conception and continues after physical death in either Heaven or Hell. Man is judged by his works. Good will works against bad will works, a moral man against an immoral man. In a positive life cycle one would attain Heaven because he worked toward and achieved being good on earth, he then attains Heaven. His soul is now in eternal happiness.

To keep a pure soul is the most important of all duties on earth to perform.

Man and His Body

The four pieces of the body - the physical body, the mind, spirit and soul - make man a united being. Man should strive to keep all parts of his body in a positive condition in the past, at present, and toward the future. To make his eternal existence possible he must be strong and good, reject evil of the physical body, thought and action of memory, of mind and soul.

If man's physical body is in handicap, due to amputation or battle, he can still attain Heaven. If man develops negative mind memory waves and a broken spirit, man can still attain eternal existence. The broken man can still hope and nothing can change his pure soul to impure except his will. Staying positive, he concludes his life in the four pieces of the body. Yet if the man was to have the three pieces in strength - body, mind, and spirit - but have an impure soul, he would be determined to go to Hell.

Henceforth, the most important intentional goal in life, above all, is to keep and maintain a pure, moral soul.

Chapter IV

The Building of Man

Giving Spiritual Will to God

Man is procreated by another man and a woman; a new soul is born. The new soul is created by God to bring pleasure to God. It is the duty of the Mother and Father to always guide the newborn in the positive path of life.

At anticipated conception the body and soul of the baby is given in prayer to God, or while the baby is still in the womb. After birth, the baby's will is given to God. When the being is old enough in age and knows his will, he gives his everlasting, eternal will to the service of God, a third time.

After the third giving, the given will to God never ends, nor does infinity.

Building the Physical Body

When the child is of age to engage in activities to build his physical muscles, endurance and stamina, he must:

- Sleep to Crawl

- Crawl to Walk

- Walk to Jog

- Jog to Sprint

- Sprint to Jog

- Jog to Walk

- Walk to Crawl

- Crawl to Sleep

Man must walk beyond his purpose to gain enduring strength. If one has to walk a mile to gain greater health and physical strength, then he should not walk only one mile, but more.

If one can jog a mile's distance, at ease, then he should not stop at what is easy. He should jog more, and afar, to what is reasonably strenuous and enhancing to the body.

If one masters a sprint of a certain distance, then he should not continue with that distance in itself. He shall make a further distance and master it.

Then after mastering that distance, master another, until he is master of all his capacity.

Gaining physical endurance and stamina is of utmost importance. One should not be bound, nor say he can do only what his body allows him. He is to be master of his body and tell his body what to do and achieve, not let his body be master over him.

Building muscle tone should be done to include the use of every muscle of the body from toes to neck - in walking, running, lifting objects, and swimming.

Weights of external material should be used to build up muscle tone of the body. Yet external weight is not always reliable and is material that is not of one's body. It is better that one can lift, push or pull his own body weight around to increase body perfection, than to rely on foreign material. Swimming increases one's endurance, stamina, and uses all the body muscles at once, making swimming and exercise in water an ultimate exercise.

One can never rely on another person to motivate oneself. Nor can one rely on weights or water to improve his physical body. One must reach within his own self and always strive to improve toward perfection. One must run or push or pull his own body weight to gain utmost internal strength.

Warming of the Body

When one sleeps, one should sleep in contentment and not be harshly bothered or shook. When awakening, one should go through the process of awakening gradually. After one awakens, he then notices his surroundings. He is now conscious, but should not get out of his bed place until the third level of awakening. On the third level of awakening, which is the realization of the day anew, one shall sit up in his bed for a number of minutes, warming his body gradually for the new day. Then getting up in a positive attitude for the day to come.

One must awaken gradually, not be startled or awaked suddenly, because it is bad for the body and produces a negative force of abnormality in the body for that waking day.

In physical activity, to gain muscle tone, one shall warm his body, stretching his body slowly to a level of exercise. Pacing higher to gain that muscle tone, then back down at the end of the complete exercise. Pacing himself back down from physical height to physical rationale at an existing level before the exercise.

At the end of a day one should not immediately engage himself in his bed place to sleep. Rather he should unload the pressure gradually resting then on his decision of right body adaptability preparing for his bed place, warm down his body in complete silence a few minutes, then go to sleep.

A man shall awaken, not by force, but when the body feels it needs to awaken; when it has had enough rest and is ready for a new day, every day.

Hot and Cold Temperature Tolerance

Man shall not be bound by any physical or non-physical substance within the universe. Man is greater than all within the universe, except God. Man is third in line of greatness with the universe:

- First - God

- Second - Good Spirits

- Third - Man

God is omnipresent, not always physical, only at His choice is He.

Good spirits gain physical appearance at God's will.

God has willed that man always be of physical body and form.

Earth is a physical property for man to live on.

Day and night are of variety and of purposeful situation.

Hot and cold are temperatures that effect the physical body of man.

Man is above all on the earth, he shall not fear anything within the universe, except that to which just fear is attributed. When it is dark, man shall walk in that dark to overcome any and all fear of it. So that when he travels in the dark he will know he has overcome any fear of it, and pass through it until a lighted path comes at twilight.

In the winter when it is cold and the wind blows and the sky rains, hails, and snows, man shall experience at least one time walking with little clothing into the elements. Abiding in it until he can almost no longer stand it and a little longer. He will no longer fear it and his body will realize the truth of the elements and he shall have conquered these.

In the summer heat, man will put his body to exist about the hot sun to his capability, and a little longer. So that he might know the truth of the summer sun, experiencing it at its hottest, he shall overcome the sun and will not fear summers to come.

Man exists over nature and man conquers over all, therefore in a time and safe manner:

When it is hot, man shall bathe in hot water and then in cold.

When it is cold, man shall bathe in cold water, and then in hot.

When it is hot, man shall drink hot water, and later cold.

When it is cold, man shall drink cold water, and later hot.

Making a physical immunity unto his own body, man becomes immune to temperature, yet lives in contentment with temperature. Man conquers all, internally and externally.

Nutrition

God made earth for his pleasure. God made man for his pleasure. Man needs food to survive. God supplies man with nutrition to keep man alive.

- Water to drink.

- Fruits and vegetables to eat.

- Animals to eat.

- Fish to eat.

A man with a pure body and soul has attained, through purity, good perception. Therefore, he should know by sight, and feeling within, what food to eat:

- Drink clean, clear water, not dirty.

- Eat fruit and vegetables that are clean, and are not blemished.

- Eat animals or fish that live a good life and are clean, and are not scavengers or blemished.

One should only eat that which he feels good about. Only putting into his internal being what is of a good nature, not of a bad nature. If one puts impure food into his body he can only expect his mind, body, and soul to deplete in a negative fashion toward evil, and effects the genes of next generations to come.

If one eats good, clean food, he is positive.

If one eats bad, unclean food, he is negative.

The body can only be as strong as one makes it, and as strong as his ancestors' genes have been. Therefore, in nutrition one shall eat what one needs to stay constantly healthy. Man shall not become weakened by hunger, nor shall man be controlled by hunger. One shall eat all the nutrients he needs to conquer all. One shall eat what his body requires and a little more.

In Nutrition

One shall eat foods that are balanced:

- Liquids - of water and juices.

- Solids - of fruit and vegetables, meat and bread.

One must avoid sweet substances of sugar or other substances unhealthy to the body. He might eat sugars at times, but not regularly.

One shall nourish his body with proteins, making his being strong, not weak; decisive, not indecisive.

One can only desire of oneself that which one prepares for oneself. One either makes his being weak or strong, it is up to his will.

The man of nutrition conquers all, for his body is confident and not in hunger, he desires nothing, he is a positive force.

Fasting and Purity of Internal Organs

According to a man's degree of ability, one shall fast to cleanse his body and gain strength:

- 1 day of the week up to 12 hours.

- 1 day, of night and day, once every three months

- 3 days, of night and day, two times every year.

One shall take natural juices, or hot water, to cleanse one's kidneys and bowels, when necessary or during fasting.

He that desires to attain purity and Heaven must keep a clean, pure internal physical body.

External Purity

Man's physical body shall be bathed in continuously running water. Man should bathe in running water and use soap-like substances at least once a day, to rid his body of bodily poisons and foreign matter. While washing, one shall wash his hair and all other parts of his body from hair to toes.

A salt bath shall be taken at least twice a year. One should soak his body for five to ten minutes in gathered warm water to which a hand of salt has been added. The salt draws poisons out of the body, therefore purifying the body. Then afterwards rinse his body with regular water.

Bath of Spiritual Purity

A bath to purify one's being of evil spirits shall be taken in a bath of gathered warm water after one has already taken a soap bath. This bath should include water that has been blessed in the name of God, and has a hand of tobacco added to the water. One shall remain in the bath for five to ten minutes, with the intention of ridding oneself of the physical and spiritual properties evil spirits. This bath enables good spirits, then, to dwell within and about one's being.

This bath may be taken preventatively three times a year, or when spiritually necessary.

Smoking

The tobacco and cedar shall first be blessed in the name of God before it is used.

To rid a person or an environment of bad spirits, or to keep good spirits with a person or an environment, one shall:

- Burn tobacco on a container until it smokes.

- Burn cedar on a container until it smokes.

- Then bless the person and/or environment with the smoke.

- Smoke tobacco in a pipe while striving not to inhale.

The smoking of tobacco or cedar shall be done in either the prevention or rebuking of evil spirits; and should be done for a person or an environment once every three months, or whenever spiritually necessary.

Body of One

The body is the temple of God and shall be kept clean, pure and healthy at all times. When one attains purity of body and mind, he is pleasing to God; God may dwell to a greater degree in this body. This one is preparing to attain eternal existence with God through pure actions of the Body. Now if this purity is constant and remains that way, one is one with God and God may dwell in the body of this pure human eternally.

Chapter V

Thoughts and Actions of the Body

Right and Wrong

After one is born and is growing in maturity and in age, one always seeks to do what is right and what is good. Humans are basically of a good nature and seek to do what is pleasing to God.

There is a right way to do things and there is a wrong way. One of a pure mind shall know right from wrong without being told. The feeling of decision-making between these two choices in innate. Therefore, one shall know right from wrong by his own trusted feelings, and does not need to be told by others.

Faults

Man is not perfect. Each person must continuously strive toward perfection in his life in order to attain eternal existence.

One who faults in his daily life of decision or action, has nothing more important to do than to realize his fault, acknowledge it, and strive to improve himself. Thereby, eventually overcoming and conquering all faults of thought and action.

Sin

One must realize his faults before they become sins, because, once in sin, man affects and dements his: Mind, Body, Spirit, Soul, and Eternity.

The mind is consciously or unconsciously filled with guilt and knows what it has done wrong. The mind becomes confused and illogical in other forms of decision making in the future.

The body may feel the thought and action of sin throughout the body, becoming emotionally and/or physically sick and weak.

The soul is affected by sin and the good spirit of one dements. Once the soul dements, the soul lessens in purity and weakens to further sin.

The eternity of one is affected by sin. One becomes bad, not necessarily thoroughly, but in instances of actions. If innumerable serious sins occur, the eternity of one is doubtful in attaining Heaven.

One must avoid sin at all times. Go not to places where sin is to be found. Go not with people who encourage sin. One must think for himself and not rely on the thoughts of others totally for making decisions. One knows right from wrong and must act accordingly in every moment of the day, in every environment and in every situation.

Confession of Sin

When one sins, he knows he has sinned by his own feeling. He must, on that first act of sin so that it may not continue, confess his sin:

- First to God

- Second to Himself

- Third to family or friend, or Spiritual Leader.

Acknowledging in the mind and by word, one realizes his wrong action or thought. In confession one actually rejects what he had done, admits it and strives in the future not to repeat it.

Confession is good for the mind, body, spirit, and soul of man. Confession of wrongdoings makes a humble man and a strong man; confession does not weaken him nor do his sins compound; so that in strength one might be one with God.

Diminishing Highs

One shall not indulge himself in the life of temporary highs - highs that might make one feel as though he is having fun or important. Any short-term high that is wrong and dements a being. One shall avoid and not involve himself in deviant and sinful acts as:

- Immoral sex

- Gambling

- Chemical inducement to the body

- Lying

- Thievery

- Other acts of the senses of action as: thinking, looking, touching, smelling, and eating

If one finds himself, or others, involved in such action, he shall leave that environment and confess his wrongdoing. There is no fun in fault or sin, it only dements the being and hurts God.

Natural Highs

One shall, to gain happiness in mind and body, indulge himself in natural highs:

Encounters of Man:

- Family friendships

- Friends

- Lovemaking: man to woman, woman to man

Encounters of Natural Earth:

- Plant life and environment of Earth

- Animals in contentment

Encounters of the Day:

- Listening

- Talking

- Learning

- Eating

- Exercising

- Skill interests

- Adventure

- Dance and song

- Thinking

- Expressing or realizing the Love of Life

- Love of Life

- Other

Natural highs are intermittently constant, never ending. Whatever good choice of a natural high, they are the purest of thought and action; there is no sin in them if done properly.

Natural highs allow the mind and body to feel good; the relief making a more positive being as each day lapses.

Race and Culture

God created the universe, the earth and man. He did not create one type of tree or one shade of water, but many different varieties. Therefore, it is logical that man has different languages and various shades of color. God is content with different varieties of the earth and cultures, it is pleasing to Him in different ways. One culture may have a superior attribute over another, but all have some good contributions to please God in different ways.

Different cultures should strive to appreciate variety and the attributes of each other and, if at all possible, to live in contentment with one another and God.

Nature in Harmony

It is proposed that man and the earth are to be in harmony and contentment with the will of God.

When God is content, man may be content.

When man needs water and it is taken, water and man are content.

When man needs shelter and it is used, space is content.

When man needs woman, and woman needs man, they are content.

When nature is in need of its purposeful motion, all creation is existing in harmony.

Harmony can only be attained by each creation performing the will of God, and the harmonious purpose thereof.

Earth

Earth is everything from air to water, dirt to rocks, plants, animals, insects, and man. Everything that is a part of earth is made from earth. Everything that lives on earth, survives off another part of the earth. Everything that lives on earth eventually dies and becomes part of earth again.

There is a beginning and an end to everything, except God. God created earth in the beginning, and earth shall be replaced and cease in the end.

God is the only spectrum of life that has ever infinitely lived and shall forever live. Every other creation and element of the universe is subject to His will to exist, and will cease if, and when, it is His will.

Part Two

The Seventeen Books

of Wisdom

Chapter VI

The First Book of Wisdom:

The Laws of Life

Laws of Life

Laws of Life to live by are made not to be broken. Each Person of society is taught the laws from birth to an age until he reaches an expression of teaching another. Man knows right from wrong inately. Laws of Life are inate laws, and are logical to a sane society.

If Laws of Life are broken, there are three degrees of punishment:

- Death

- Banishment

- Correction

Acts of Death

The acts that require the punishment of death are:

- Worship of gods, rather than one God

- Witches

- Blasphemy

- All forms of sodomy

- Orgy

- Incest

- Insane murder

- Oral copulation

- Cannibalism, or introductory cannibalism

- Insanity

- Killing without reason

- Sadism and masochism

- Bestiality

- Abuse of children or others, sexually or physically

- Homosexuality

- Other determined acts

These acts are considered worse than sin. Any man or woman involved in just one of these acts was to be:

- Put to death.

- The physical body is burnt to ashes.

- The clothing, shelter, and all belongings of this person burnt to ashes. Nothing of this person is to be kept by anyone.

- The physical body ashes are to be taken far from the Tribal environment and buried deep in the ground.

- The environmental ashes are to be taken far from the Tribal environment and buried deep in the ground.

If a man was judged guilty and to be put to death by a majority vote taken among a court of Tribal Chiefs and/or Chieftains. After the sentence of death was determined, three executioners would take the man to a private place with no direct onlooker and kill him. One or two out of the three executioners would do the killing and the other executioner was there to oversee the accomplishment of the act.

A small contingent of Adults and Tribal Chiefs and Chieftains observe the event to insure it was taking place correctly, and to prevent any unusual developmental behavior patterns of the executioners.

Family members of the person executed would not hold future grudges against the executioners since they are only doing their duty for the Tribe; nor would it be talked about, nor told who, of the three executioners, performed the specific act. Life has ended at death, and death was performed quickly, not torturously.

Acts of Death or Punishment

There are some acts that may be given the judgment of death or banishment from the Tribe, which is determined by the Tribal Chief(s) and/or Chieftains:

- Rape

- Lying

- Theft

- Gossip

- Other detrimental acts.

Acts that result in either death or banishment are judged upon by how many times they are committed and whether they were for justifiable reasons. If the act continues after repeated correction, the man is either banished from the Tribal environment and grounds, or he is put to death.

Acts of Correction

Acts that are judged to need correction are:

- Personal hygiene

- Dishonesty

- A non-virtuous person

- Material desire

- Life without wisdom

- Laziness

- Pride

- Other determined acts

Once a person is reprimanded in acts of correction, he shall show improvement. If no improvement is made or is not desired by that person, he shall then be banished. Once banished, a person is seldom, if ever, allowed to return to the Tribe, and others may choose to leave with him.

Pure Society

The Laws of Life might seem severe to persons of another society, but a mass of pure beings is better than a mass of sinful, contaminated beings. Unenforced laws allow a society to become corrupted by too much leniency, and civilization will soon cease. God will leave a corrupt environment;

therefore, to keep God in society, man must control and do away with uncontrollable impure man.

A society without evil is a society of purity, one that God can look upon and be pleased with. His Creations should live a life that pleases Him.

Judgment of Laws

Judgment upon one is carried out by a Council of Chieftains making a decision about the questionable act of that person.

If a Chieftain, mother or father, brother or sister, any relative or warrior acts in a wrong way, he is to be judged upon just as any other person. There is no favoritism of:

- A Chieftain of another Chieftain or relative

- A Father of a son or daughter

- A Mother of a son or daughter

- Children to parents

- A Husband of a wife

- A Friend of a friend

- A Warrior of a warrior

- Other acquaintances

Laws are set and absolute, all being of intended purity. All persons judged to be impure receive the same appropriate retribution regardless of his status.

In Acts of Death

A child conceived and/or born during acts that are punishable by death shall also receive death at birth or in the womb of that woman.

Hereditary sin is to be stopped at its source, and no child could be pure that is born during impure acts. Therefore, it is better that he die than be allowed to live and later corrupt society.

In Acts of Death or Banishment

If a man is in anger: If a man's sister or relative is raped and the man kills the person that did the rape, then nothing shall happen to him.

If a person causes havoc and dismay in society by serious lying, and/or dishonors another person(s) with untruthful gossip and is killed by that person(s), nothing shall be done to the killer(s) if the killing was determined to be right by the Tribal Chieftains and Chief(s).

If one kills another for stealing something of only material value and no purposeful use, the man who has killed another, without just cause, shall either be banished or receive death. But if one steals the food of another, or

47

medicine of life, and this person dies from such an act, and the thief is killed by a friend or relative, nothing shall be done to that person.

In Acts of Correction

If one does not improve in acts of correction after a given time period, and has not passed from family correction to Tribal correction levels, he shall be banished. This is because:

- Personal hygiene not taken seriously can result in an unclean being. When unclean and contaminated, his behavior patterns will become deviate.

- A dishonest person is not only dishonorable, but also disastrous to society.

- An unvirtuous person is a person without goal or purpose in life and only brings evil to society.

- A person with unyielding material desire is a fool of life. He strives not toward God, but toward matter of no eternal value.

- A life without wisdom is a life without rule or cause; thus one may only expect disaster for himself and society.

- A lazy person is of no value to himself or society.

- A person of pride is a fool, who walks the way of personal envy without helping others in society, which leads to thinking about himself before God.

Persons that need correction should act accordingly, lest they allow one fault to lead them into another fault, from fault to deviance, from deviance to sin, from sin to acts punishable by banishment or death, to death itself. A person should take a correction in humility and improve thereof.

In Genetic Cause

Any man, as a child or thereafter, who is born with or develops a serious mental illness or retardation of the mind shall be put to death by the executioner; as shall any man, as a child or thereafter, who is born with serious blemishes or a physical handicap of the body. These persons disrupt the Genetic Cause of man's genes, they are abnormal and disrupt the genetic pattern of man. Thus it is best to extinguish disruptive genes than to have a society of dysfunctional humans and handicapped persons in the future.

No person or society is, nor has ever been, perfect; but man should strive toward perfection. God Himself is perfect; humans can never attain perfection, but can strive towards perfection as well as strive to please God, as one, and as a society.

Chapter VII

Second Book of Wisdom: Building of Wisdom

Heredity

Just as one born receives the physical characteristics of one's parents, so he also receives some portion of the spiritual, moral, talent, wisdom and intellectual characteristics of his parents.

Therefore, if parents are pure, without sin, and are wise in life, so should the child be. But if faults are present in the parents, the child shall work to alleviate such tendencies.

Human Life: 0-100 Years of Age

Formulas for the development of a wise man:

0 years:

- Pure parents in love at conception.

- Interaction of life with baby while in the womb.

- Blessing of baby in the womb to serve God in his life.

0-5 years:

- Taught right from wrong.

- Child spoken to numerous times on rules of life and the wisdom of life. A child may not comprehend at this age, but beliefs are placed in his mind in the foundation years of life.

- Parent(s), and other Tribal members, listen to the new ideas and wisdom of the new generation.

5-10 years:

- Verbal and nonverbal preparation for death and eternity with God.

- Taught Laws of Life.

- Taught love and hate.

- Honor and dishonor.

- Life and death.

- Taught hunting and fighting tactics.

- Friends are made and kept.

- Virtues of man taught.

10-15 years:

- Reinforcement of Laws of Life.

- Love and hate.

- Actual and continuing hunting, alertness toward dangers in life, and warfare tactics.

- Sexual realization, man to woman, woman to man.

- Concepts of husband and wife.

- Concepts of marriage and marriage if willed.

- Taught wisdom of life and judgments.

- Virtues of man continued.

15-20 years:

- Total knowledge and realization of Laws of Life.

- Care of wife(s) and children.

- Realization of man's place in society.

- Wisdom attained.

20-25 years:

- Wisdom in growth.

- Continuation of all taught, 0-25 years.

- Purifications of the mind, body and soul.

25-50 years:

- Wise man.

- Continuation of all taught, 0-50 years.

50-100 years:

- Absolute wise man.

- Continuation of all taught, 0-100 years.

- Complete preparation for physical death and eternity with God.

Perfection of the Young

A child is born of purity, and pure is what all men shall strive to be. A child by conscience knows right from wrong, love, hate, honor and dishonor, by being born of purity and without rare fault and serious sin.

A child strives to do what is right and pleasing. He desires to be happy, not sad. A child is human perfection. In fact, a child is the best result of God's Creation of life from man and woman combined.

The parents, in purity, make a better human than they themselves are. A man shall want his sons and daughters to be greater than he. A woman shall want her sons and daughters to be greater than herself so the child might be more pleasing to God.

Therefore, the young are a main purpose in life and their perfection of life is guided by God, mother, father, relatives, and society.

Children are listened to, looked up to, and learned from, not discredited; because in birth and aging they are to be a better generation of human perfection.

Children are taught by elders the Laws of Life. But, in fact, they are to become the new elders in years to come and shall treat the new young the same.

Each generation of the Caddo is a progressing perfection of man, to please God individually and as a society.

Young, Middle and Old Aged

In wise thought: The old were once young, whom now grow old. The old are dying. The young are growing to middle aged. The middle aged are growing old. The middle aged are procreating more young.

A wise man does not judge another by his chronological physical age, rather by his mental, emotional and spiritual age. A wise man judges a man by the sum total of these demonstrated traits. A wise man realizes that he will soon pass through all ages of life; appreciating each moment in life at every age. However, he may not attain or reach, in life, the desired demonstrated traits of a wise man, even though he may grow chronologically old in age.

A wise man does not live, or judge, by chronological time, rather he lives in time, and makes the best use of his time in life to attain an eternal existence with God.

Chapter VIII

Third Book of Wisdom: Virtues of Man

Life of Virtue

A virtuous man strives to do what is correct in life. He ideally has a good conscience from conception and birth. Man seeks pleasure and peace of mind. Therefore, in wisdom, he realizes his mind and is honest with it. He, by wisdom, realizes positive and negative forces in life; realizing fault, sins, and virtue. One set of actions destroys man, another set builds man.

Virtues

The definitions of the different virtues are:

- Love and Hate: To love what is good, to hate what is evil.

- Morality: To realize a sexual need, and rules of standard. Realize that normal sex is good, and immoral sex is evil.

- Purity: Man is to keep pure thoughts because they lead to action to sustain a pure mind, body and soul.

- Honesty: Man is to be honest with himself and others.

- Kindness: Man is kind to all ages of man and to animals and all of the earth.

- Charity: When one sees another in need of help, to help that person uplift himself.

- Bravery: It is good to act brave, yet not as a fool and endanger one's life just for the act of bravery itself.

It is not only through realization of these and other virtues that a man attains wisdom, but he must act and do what is right and act out his wise thoughts.

It is a positive force to act virtuous, but negative to not act in virtuous ways. It is a fault, in itself, to see and not act virtuous.

Therefore, one must always act sincerely to gain the grace of God that He might enlighten the mind to further wisdom.

Man attains Heaven through acts of wisdom, not through the mere knowledge of wisdom and virtues.

Chapter IX

Fourth Book of Wisdom: Social Class

God

Above all and everything is God. All persons, within order of the universe, first regard God, then themselves, then others. All men are not procreated equal; each man makes his own life, either for better or worse, as he acts by his will.

Chief(s) and Chieftain Rulers

Rulers of the Tribe are those continually born into the hereditary ruling family. There is a set order by which the hereditary ruler ship is passed down from one generation to the next.

- If only one son is born to a man and woman: In the years after attaining wisdom he may join in the rule with his father and/or mother. After their death he remains in rule or begins to rule.

- If two or more sons are born to a man and a woman: The sons, after attaining wisdom, help in rule of the Tribe(s). The wisest, most spiritual and multi-ability son ranks supreme.

If more that one sons(s) and/or daughter(s) are born to a man and a woman: After attaining wisdom they help as a family in rule of the Tribe(s).

In Caddo life there is a single Supreme Chief, but also other Chief(s) and Chieftains to help rule the Tribe. The Chieftains rule over the Tribe as a body of judgment on different issues. The man who is purest, most wise, and perpetually seeks to attain and preserve the indwelling of God, and sustains this mode is ranked supreme. He is the Head Supreme Chief of the Caddo Tribes.

Judgments of Chief(s) and Chieftains

It is the duty of a Chieftain to oversee and pass judgments on every aspect of Tribal life.

A Chieftain:

Judges Individuals

- A person's purity

- A person's Honor

Judges Tribal Affairs

- Peace

- Time of War

- Time of Travel

- Time of Tribal Purification

- Tribal Domestic and Foreign Policy

Judges Criminal Acts

- Acts of Death

- Acts of Correction

- Acts of Banishment

Judges Family Affairs

- Husband to Wife (or Wives)

- Wife (or Wives) to Husband

- Father to Children

- Mother to Children

- Marriage(s) and Separation

Judges Cause and Effect of Repetitive Actions

- On the Universe

- On the Ecology

- On the Earth

Judges His Environment

- His Friends

- His Allies

- His Enemies

- His Traditions

- His Tribe and/or Tribal Band's Lifestyle

Judges and Determines the Economy

- Commerce

- Trade Routes

- Bartering Service Methods and Measures

- Trade and Service with Other Tribes

- Regulation of Economy

- Hunting and Agriculture

Judges other determined acts and instances of life.

Chief(s) and Chieftains

Chief(s) and Chieftain and his family rank above all others of the Tribe. A Chieftain realizes the duties of his position, accepts them, and then acts accordingly. He is to be pure, moral, and wise to obtain oneness with God. A Chieftain is not proud of himself or position, but rather has pride within himself. A Chieftain is humble and kind, not haughty, nor does he seek the destruction of others for reasons of jealousy or revenge or power.

Masculine and Feminine

Masculine

A masculine man is the most superior creation of all created by God on earth. A masculine man is:

- Pure

- Moral

- Kind

- Just

- Talented

- Decisive

- Knows his Sexuality

- Fine Countenance

- Honorable

- Degree of Athletics

- Body in Tone

- Of Fine Mannerisms, Stance, and Walk

- A Degree of Being a Warrior

- A Good Husband

- A Good Father

- One with God

- Other

A masculine man seeks the environmental comfort and love of a feminine woman or women.

Feminine

A feminine woman is the second most superior creation created by God on earth. A feminine woman is:

- Pure

- Moral

- Kind

- Just

- Talented

- Decisive

- Knows Her Sexuality

- Fine Countenance

- Honorable

- Body in Tone

- Of Fine Mannerisms, Stance, and Walk

- A Good Wife

- A Good Mother

- One with God

- Other

A feminine woman seeks the environmental comfort and love of a masculine man or men.

A Mother and a Father

There is no one greater than a good Mother and/or a good Father, for they are the basis of all generations to come.

A Mother and a Father together procreate the race and strive to perfect man.

A Mother

A woman in marriage to; man knows her responsibility and, if so desired, to bear children and take care of them both physically and spiritually. A Mother knows the Laws of Life and lives by them and so teaches her children. A Mother is virtuous. A Mother is strict yet kind. A Mother is firm yet reasonable. A Mother is a life long friend and guide to her children - eternally. A Mother is One with God.

A Father

A man in marriage to a woman knows his responsibility and, if so desired, to produce children and take of them both physically and spiritually. A Father knows the Laws of Life and lives by them and so teaches his children. A Father is virtuous. A Father is strict yet kind. A Father is firm yet reasonable. A father is a lifelong friend and guide to his children - eternally. A Father is One with God.

Brothers and Sisters

Brothers and/or Sisters shall respect one another, not be jealous, and shall always endeavor to love and defend one another. If another person unjustly wrongs one's Brother or Sister, he shall make it his duty to bring them to proper justice. Brothers and Sisters shall always care for one another in health or in sickness, and shall always care for the life of each other's children, both physically and spiritually.

Friends

Friends shall be made and kept eternally, but shall break the bond of friendship if the friend is intentionally unjust to one or one's relative. Friends shall always care for one another in youth and in old age. A good friend is one of the greatest gifts from God that a man can have. Friends include: oneself, relatives, and non-relatives.

Warriors

A Warrior

A Warrior shall be pure and confident in fighting ability. He shall have an in-tone body, great stamina and speed. He shall hate the evil and/or the action of the enemy, love oneself and Tribe. A warrior before battle shall be knowledgeable of the reasons for battle and its justifiability.

A Warrior must be brave and think of his tactics and alternatives before battle in order to predict and counteract the enemy's tactics. A Warrior must be wise and have no fear of death, yet have a great desire to live since that is why he battles in wars.

Warriors in Social Class

Warriors are not ranked on how brave they are or how many men they have killed nor how fearless they are, because war is an act of hate. Love is the basis of life, not hate. Therefore, warriors are ranked neither higher nor lower in class since they only serve a duty of the Tribe.

In fact, fathers, and sons are all warriors when need be. So there is no praise in a warrior's actions, it is something expected of him. No man shall take pleasure or pride in the death of another, even though the other is his enemy. A true warrior has sorrow for the death of another man, although thoughts of sorrow are gone in seconds.

The act of war, and action of warriors, is enacted to retain the life and vitality of the Tribe. A warrior fights because he loves himself and Tribe, not because he loves to kill or attain position or power.

Class Structure

The three levels of Class Structure are:

- High Class

- Middle Class

- Low Class

Class is not judged by material wealth nor gain nor promise. Material wealth is undesirable to a man content and wise within his own mind and being. Nor is one judged on his accomplishments or achievements, although they are recognized.

In fact, a man is judged in class by his purity, wisdom, and relation with God. Nothing else really exists or matters. Therefore, humans are judged only as:

- Supreme Chief

- Chief(s)

- Chieftains

- Mothers and Fathers

- Brothers and Sisters

- Friends

- Tribal Member

Persons within the tribal environment serve different ranks of social class duties, although the higher, middle, and lower classes may intermix and neither is discriminated against. The classes are a part of a hierarchical higher class system with respect and interaction to the lower and middle classes, because persons within all three classes can attain degrees of purity and the indwelling of God. These classes may also move up in class by marriage, achievement, and by proving themselves worthy. All classes serve a purpose in the tribal atmosphere. Everyone is interdependently respected and needed.

Structure of Political and Religious Hierarchy

Among the Caddo

Supreme Chief

Superior Chiefs   Form a

Religious Leaders   Council of

Chieftains   Chieftains

Chapter X

Fifth Book of Wisdom:

Humans of Eternal Thought

One to God

To be One with God, one must be One to God. Meaning that each person, to maintain a pure mind and soul, must strive to think in his personal action as God would think. Humans must act, and speak, as though they are under close supervision of God. To attain a better after life one must act as though he is already there, acting as he would if he was in Heaven. This way, one's actions are motivated to be good at all times, not fluctuating nor varying.

Humans must think of God as within and as a friend who is always beside man in spirit and shares in the life of each man. Man is one to God if he strives to share each moment of the day with Him as a friend, and thinking how He might judge and act in a situation. Therefore, man imagines his mind to be inset with God. In this mode of thought man grows mentally and spiritually and becomes better. After a time, this practice of concentration lapses and man's actions become one with God.

Family to God

The family unit must be united as one; brothers and sisters should love and care for one another. Husband(s) and wife (or wives) shall act in the same manner. A loving family is pleasing to God and this family shall exist intact eternally if the members aspire and attain Heaven.

Tribe to God

The Tribe shall love and serve God; all actions should be thought in the favor of God. A Tribe that gives such respect to God is favored and cherished eternally. The Chief(s) and Chieftains must strive to keep the Tribe pure within the eyes of God. Family members must act morally and be of a sincere manner.

Eternal Actions

Actions done in the service of God are just, but actions done just to gain favor from God's grace are insincere and unjust. Therefore, humans, of eternal thought, will act purely to please God and to perfect themselves, not just for eternal favor from God. To act sincerely in a pure manner is the method by which oneself, family, and Tribe shall attain the love of God and eternal happiness.

Chapter XI

Sixth Book of Wisdom:

The Working Society

One-half of the day is light and one-half of the day is dark. Different duties and tasks for the family are done at the necessary times. Duties, such as cleaning and preparation of food, are done during the day in daylight. While other duties are done during the night. Work and playing of athletic games might be done during the day, while tribal dances and socializing with friends might be done during the night. Hunting of game or gathering or vegetables, grains and fruits, as well as farming would be a task of the day; as would cleaning of the tribal grounds.

The meaning of the working society is to function in a disciplined manner. Man must know what to do at what time of the day and what not to do at the other. Society must work in a synchronized fashion, goals must be individually set and achieved in certain time frames.

When the hunt is over or when food is obtained, the women must be ready in time to prepare the meal. The children must be through playing in time to eat. The Tribe must be ready to start the dance at the same time. Life rotates in a circular fashion. What tasks are performed today might be the same as yesterday and tomorrow. Each person in the working society knows his place and his duties and acts accordingly.

The working society is in harmony with each person. The society is one of balance of work, play, care, and prayer. A society must stay in harmony to survive; for once the society is out of order, the path is short to chaos and destruction. To avoid such peril, the society and the Chieftains must maintain order over duties and time schedules.

Chapter XII

Seventh Book of Wisdom:

The Meaning of Goals of Life

The Meaning of Life

There is limited physical meaning to life since life is essentially spiritual. Man is born, lives on and of the earth, then dies. Another man is born and repeats the same process. This physical process measures life, giving value to the spiritual. Life, then, is measured in an eternal context in relation with God. God chooses to create man and gain pleasure from him. When God is pleased with the way a man lives, this specific man gains favor and might attain Heaven. If God is displeased, he might go to Hell.

There is no real meaning to man himself, only his physical motion of everlasting repetitiveness of playing, sleeping, eating, and working. The ingredient of life that has meaning is man's caring thought and moral action;

thought-and-action is life. Life, totally, is not what we physically taste or smell, hear or feel. Life is choosing between right and wrong and the reasoning behind our choices. Our physical body helps discern our decisions through the perception of the senses, which we then make choices by moral reasoning. And it is these choices that make up life, an eternal life of the soul.

The Goals of Life

After one has attained the age of ten, and thereafter, he must set goals to guide his life. Physical goals are such things as physical improvement of the body; and spiritual goals are goals of mental development. Goals to God are set to develop one's lifestyle that one might attain Heaven. When one knows one's path, he wants to follow it and he rarely deviates from that path. Man must open his mind to thoughts of spiritual wisdom from his elders so that his goals may not be far-fetched, but reasonable and attainable, and yet use his judgment and unique decisions.

In setting goals in one's mind, man achieves mental happiness; he is not confused nor misguided; he knows right from wrong, not through mere dogma, but through logical reasoning.

Reasoning logically on small problems to large is a task that must be learned through years of constant thought. One must know how to reason logically to remain mentally capable of Heaven.

Man achieves reason through constantly setting goals to figure out a problem by himself, and/or discuss it with a peer, an elder, to a logical conclusion.

Happiness within the mind can only be attained through the setting of goals and doing chosen tasks which bring about the desired potential end result. In logic one will find happiness. Within the mental motivation of happiness is the cyclical method of problem solving, and man may achieve his goals. Without set goals, man's mind wanders off into laziness and dissipation into evil.

Short-term goals are primary and prepare the foundation for long-term goals. Just as a narrow path is followed to avoid danger, man must follow a narrow path in life because once he deviates from the path, and wanders, he might never find the path again and perish.

Chapter XIII

Eighth Book of Wisdom:

Judgment of Oneself and Others

Man must continually strive to achieve perfection by judging and evaluating his own actions and those of others around him. A wise man spends five minutes at the beginning of the day thinking of his daily goals; and five minutes at the end of the day evaluating and improving his performance of those goals. One also spends time evaluating his verbal speech and methods of action, and the improvement of his physical and mental abilities.

A wise man judges himself and others, not on material worth, nor athletic or battle accomplishment, but on moral virtues. Virtues of the heart and soul: understanding, kindness, humility, speech, manners, moral integrity, etc. A true man would possess such characteristics as well as being good to his family and Tribe, while at the same time teaching others to attain a like greatness of the soul and love of God. These virtues are those which instill happiness in the mind and soul, and those which one should look for in himself and others.

When these virtues are lacking, one must improve if he wishes to attain Heaven. Therefore, in order to reach perfection, a man must balance his time and perform his daily goals at the necessary times. A man should not work all the time, nor should he play all the time. A man of wisdom knows what to do, when it is to be done, and acts accordingly.

In judging other men and their mistakes, one must first know the other man's limitations as well as his own. One must place himself mentally and emotionally in the life experience of the other man in order to judge his actions and the consequential results.

Chapter XIV

Ninth Book of Wisdom:

Thoughts of Logic and Wisdom

Man needs time to contemplate ideas and resolve questions in his mind in order to come to the correct conclusion. It is a wise man that uses reason and logic in making decisions; this, in fact, is the only way to make decisions. One should strive to avoid making rash or emotional decisions. Logic to the Caddo is both deductive reasoning as well as anticipating the future results of thoughts and actions, and the consequences thereof.

Before a man moves from where he is, he first must know where he is going. First he must contemplate, then act upon what is decided to be the correct action. It is both unwise and illogical to act first, then think of the results later.

When a man contemplates actions and the future outcome is good and the results are positive, then he has logic and is wise. Therefore, one must think before he acts, think before he speaks, and refrain from both until he contemplates their future. It is usually the man of peace and quiet who should be followed, he is often appropriately firm and usually is both logical and wise.

Chapter XV

Tenth Book of Wisdom:

Peace and War

Peace

Our time is predominately dominated by peace. Peace of mind and soul is always to remain a constant, even at times of war. In peace we are at harmony with nature and God. In war we are in question, question of right and wrong, and in question of death. Peace is not to be broken, but if broken, remedy of action will be decided by a consensus of thought by the Supreme Chief, Chief(s) and Chieftains. After battle and war, treaties might be decided upon by the warring parties to remain at peace, and/or battle might just cease or wars may continue and never end. Wars are also fought to regain peace, and wars will be fought to maintain peace, yet tribal rights will not be subjugated - such as loss of freedoms - to establish or maintain peace.

War

Battles and wars are fought not out of glory for conquest and death, but to preserve the Tribes' religions, economic, political, and territorial interest.

Wars are to be fought to re-establish a tribal unit and retain its territory. Wars at the same time destroy nature and disperse the family of animals into the wilderness. Wars destroy territory and flesh, yet at the same time bring out the best qualities of a man and his Tribe as well as the worst. During war one strives to use those attributes he has improved upon, such as logic and athletic ability, to their greatest potential to maintain the existence of himself and the Tribe.

Preparation for War

A Tribe must always be prepared for battle and war or surprise attacks. Each person must know his place and duty. Women and children may hide, along with the elderly, while the men have already planned their method of defense and offensive action, before the battle has begun by having rehearsed these methods time and again.

In a decided upon battle and war, which necessitates travel, provisions will be carried as well as an abundance of weapons and seasonal clothing. Man will only fight in battles and wars, women will not serve at any time. However, women can help in the preparation for war, such as cooking, packing provisions and other duties to insure a stable journey.

Before going into war, the warriors will take a bath in blessed water to purify their beings, and will be smoked with cedar and/or tobacco. Warriors will confess any wrongdoings to the leading Chieftains, who will also do the same. Prayers will be said and good-byes will given to family and friends. Then the war party will be off to battle and/or war.

Warriors

The war party will consist of able-bodied men who are in good physical health and have a desire to fight. Those in bad health might help in nursing, cooking, and other tasks. Those who are able-bodied, yet do not want to fight, will not take to the warpath. The warriors will be anxious for fighting, and overcome fears of the mind, not fearing death but accepting it. More importantly, the war party will want to preserve life, life of themselves and the Tribe.

The Supreme Chief and head Chief(s) of the Tribe will not go directly into battles and wars nor will those who are next to succeed in leadership.

Their training of mind and soul is too valuable to be ended then missed, due to battle death. The Chieftains will go into battle and guide the war party in battle.

Types of War

Wars are fought to protect persons of the Tribe in certain time frames, time frames of present and the future. Battles or wars are fought, and blood is spilt for justified reasons, and to let the enemy know that such disruptive action will not be tolerated - in the present or in the future.

Wars of Principle: All wars are wars of principle, such as the taking of land or the unauthorized use of hunting grounds or taking a harvest. Wars may be waged in such cases. The killing of a man of the Tribe, who oversteps his boundary in travel for a limited period of time, is unjustified. If a man of our Tribe is killed, a war will be waged. If a man of our Tribe is taken and enslaved in another tribe, war will be waged. If a woman is raped by a man of another tribe, war will be waged. If another tribe sets fire to the harvest or kills the hunt just to cause havoc or need, war will be waged. Wars will be decided upon for other situations and reasons by the Council of Chieftains.

Defensive Wars: The Tribe shall strive to only partake in defensive wars fought when the enemy is the aggressor of territory or is the breaker of a principle. The Tribe shall strive not to invoke war but to keep peace, and not intrude on another tribe's territory or be unprincipled to another tribe.

Offensive Wars: A threat to the Tribe must first be acted upon by the enemy Tribe, which puts our Tribe in a defensive state, taking defensive action but using offensive military tactics. Offensive tactics will be used to fight the enemy and regain the territory intruded upon.

Territory: Territory shall not be gained by greedy military conquest. The use of land either for passage, hunting, or harvest will be agreed upon as neutral or participating ground by the Chief(s) and Chieftains and the other tribe's Chief(s) of two or more tribes. This will end wars or prevent them.

Battles and Wars

Short battles are to bring about a quick decisive victory, yet not total decimation to the enemy. Check-battles are a method of short hit and retreat battles to check an enemy's advance, position or retreat. The object of check battles is to disrupt and disturb the enemy force and also to show the enemy the Tribe's strength and consequences if battle persists. Agreements or treaties may then be decided upon and peace restored.

Lasting wars are constant, over a period of months, years or decades. Two or more tribes might be at war continuously, never making peace, or making peace and continuously breaking it. These wars might entail battle on and off the territory and require a constant state of war readiness. Lasting wars are not considered a peaceful way to endure life because of the need for constant defense.

When it is determined by a Council of Chieftains that a lasting war must come to an end, and it is feasible, either a War of Decimation will be waged or a War of Extermination.

Wars of Decimation are waged to reduce the men and women of another tribe to such a small number that they will no longer be a threat of the Tribe.

Wars of Extermination are waged when it is determined by the Chief(s) and Chieftains that a War of Decimation would not be enough to stop the enemy, because future generations might again start a lasting war. Therefore, extermination of a tribe, or tribes, will let it be known that the Caddo Tribe will not tolerate aggression and wars, and is not to be questioned.

Holy wars are waged by either decimation or extermination. These wars are decided upon if a group is determined to continuously engage in evil acts which offend God - such as devil worship, cannibalism, or other acts termed evil, toward the Tribe and God.

Methods of War

Defense of Territory: In the event of a surprise attack on our tribal grounds, the said warriors should already have a planned defense and counterattack. Women, children and elders will take cover in a designated area as the battle ensues. The battle should turn to an offensive battle, from a defensive battle, in order to gain the commanding role in battle.

Offensive War: The best method of battle is to attack. Do not wait for your enemy to attack you, anticipate when he will attack and attack him before he attacks you. Surprise him in the night, in the morning, while he sleeps, when he bathes or eats. Attack him and control the battle, swarm him from each side. Set fire to his belongings, kill his livestock and burn his shelter. Ambush him as he crosses the river. Ambush him on a path. Surround his area. When he goes to hunt, kill him. When he goes to fetch water, kill him.

Confuse the enemy in time of battle, let him think there are fewer warriors than there really are. Play dumb, allow him to set an ambush for you, but turn it beforehand on him. At night, light several campfires a distance apart to confuse him. Do not stay in the same camp for a long period of time. Take adequate food and medicine into battle. Do not let the enemy do to you what you might do to him. Anticipate his moves and plan yours. Send spies to watch his movements and count warriors. Learn the enemy's habits, then attack him quietly and at the right time.

Battle and Conquest

The premise of battle is to fight; in battle man dies. Either the enemy dies or we die; it is better them than us. Therefore, once battle is decided upon and engaged, death awaits.

Battles are to be won by warriors understanding the basic laws of conquest and putting them into practice:

- Not to wound an enemy, but kill him.

- Not to take any prisoners.

- Not to enslave the enemy or become a slave, but to die first.

- Not to rape women.

- Destroy the enemy's camp, but do not take his possessions.

- Have no mercy on the enemy, kill as many as possible.

- Not to take pride in the death of other men, and refrain from war stories except for purposes of improving battle methods.

- Cowards and treasonous persons will die.

Once these laws and concepts are inset in the warrior's mind, he will fight justly and without hesitation. His mind will see battle and/or war as death and devastation, with no material gain or glorious purpose. Battles are to be fought and won decisively. This can only be achieved by fighting for a just cause, by just laws, which are true and prevent chaos or a warring society.

Life and Death

Battles are to be led by those warriors most pure of mind, soul and body. Battles are won by warriors who are most fit. At times of peace man works on his being to keep in tune, and during battle he proves his worth.

After a battle is fought there are those who live and those who die. Those who live are fortunate, those who die shall either be carried back to the tribal grounds and buried or buried where determined appropriate. If time permits, and it is safe, warriors might bury the enemy's dead out of respect for man, but this is determined by time limits and which type of war is waged.

Peace After War

After battles and wars are fought and men have died, and a peaceful solution has finally been decided upon, the Tribe is at peace again. When the warriors, Chief(s) and leading Chieftains return to the tribal grounds they are greeted with prayers, dinner, and a dance. Although others may be planning burial prayers and dinners for their deceased friends and relatives.

Peace is the ultimate goal of war. Peace will be kept when there is no internal or external deviance or chaos, and if there is either, it must be quenched to again attain peace. Peace is the state of mind of God. We seek to be in harmony with Him, but this can only be achieved in totality after our enemies are crushed and our surroundings are pure.

Chapter XVI

Eleventh Book of Wisdom:

Eternity

Man lives his life for the pleasure of God and himself. Man dies on earth and his spirit either goes to Heaven or Hell. All man's actions and thoughts are performed to gain an eternity in Heaven.

Man's thoughts and actions on earth are within the same frame of time as infinite eternity. The occurrences of time in Heaven and Hell, now, are in tune with those on Earth. Meaning, Earth, Heaven, and Hell are complementary in time and one corresponds with that of another. Past, present, and future exist in all three entities of eternity.

When man dies, his spirit immediately is judged and he steps directly into the purging progressive state, or digressive state of determined eternity.

Within the mind of this deceased man exists his imaginary images of purest pleasures in Heaven and displeasures in Hell. The vivid images of artificial imagination are created and this man is subject to its physical properties, within a specific time frame and environment which are a part of his eternity.

This deceased being in Heaven or Hell might encounter past relatives or other relationships, known or unknown to him. He might also meet new friends and past enemies, spending time with either in his environment. Once in Heaven or Hell, a soul is locked in never to get out; although God might choose to extinguish a soul immediately upon death or after a period of time, or listen to pleas of remorse and then extinguish the soul.

Life is always up to God. He might put a soul in a form of Limbo, a frozen time to that being, until He determines the situation of the soul.

Man exists in the time frame of eternity from the moment his soul is conceived. God is always in eternity. God is infinite. God controls space and time, it does not control Him. God can stop time and reserve it, or speed it up if He so desires. The universe is subject to His will.

The eternity of man's body and soul is determined by himself and God. The time frame of spiritual eternity is the second progression and the last, after the first time frame on earth. In life and in death man is subject to God's judgment. Man's eternity is determined at the time of his death by his willed choices, his thoughts and actions during his entire life on earth. Man's eternity is collectively determined by himself, and is judged upon by God.

Chapter XVII

Twelfth Book of Wisdom:

Death

Man is born to live and born to die. Our future entails the end of physical life in death. We live to die, yet refrain from death by surviving to live. Man, in the spiritual favor of God, accepts death but does not entice it. The man who is evil is often scared of death because he is afraid of his eternity.

Man is made to die, he does not know when, where or how, he will die but he must be spiritually ready for judgment at all moments of life. All that man lives for, in reality, is focused toward death; his mind, soul and body are perfected during life until death and for death.

Man might die in battle, in his sleep, or due to health reasons; whichever the case, the physical transition of life to death of the body is momentary. Then the soul departs the body.

The tribal members, after the death of an individual, act according to the circumstances and have a funeral. The body is prepared with medicine then wrapped in a blanket and place in a hole as a holding place in the ground. Some of the person's personal possessions are selected and are placed in the ground with him. A ceremonial dinner is given in honor of the deceased being, and prayers are spoken in hope of a good eternity.

Chapter XVIII

Thirteenth Book of Wisdom:

Judgment of the Soul

The soul of man is judged by God immediately upon physical death.

God judges the soul of man on four separate entities:

- The Mind

- The Body

- The Soul

- The Will

The mind is judged upon thoughts of the mind from birth until death. The actions that these thoughts led to and their consequences with regard to alternatives. The mind is also judged upon intellect and wisdom, again on its sequence of thought and discernment of actions taken and consequences thereof.

The body is judged upon the physical maintenance from birth until death; whether the body was kept well nourished, or whether it was undernourished either intentionally or unintentionally, or was in physical handicap.

The mind and body are separate entities and the soul is unto itself, though all three make up a portion of one, yet the activity of the mind and body make up the soul. The soul is the spiritual unseen entity of man, the soul and will are the essence of man. Man must will himself to be good, and if need be, he must force his will to be good.

God judges the soul of man upon the main virtues of:

- Purity

- Morality

- Kindness

- Honesty

Man is to be pure in mind and thought, as well as action. Man is to maintain a clean body in an environment that is hygienic.

Man is to be moral and live the Laws of Life. If a man lives the life and Laws of Life, he will obtain wisdom and Heaven if his actions are sincere.

Man is to be kind to man, the rivers, plants, insects, animals, and not harm or pollute them. Man is to be kind in action and speech to: mother and father, husband(s) and wife(wives), son(s) and daughter(s), as well as all other beings.

Those men who have not lived a life of pure body, mind and soul, and have strayed from the life and Laws of Life, and are not moral or kind, shall receive an eternity that they have made for themselves, which is a judgment to Hell.

Chapter XIX

Fourteenth Book of Wisdom:

Eternal Happiness

Once the soul is judged upon by God to go to Heaven, the plane of happiness is also decided upon by God. The better the man, the better his eternity and eternal happiness. Man might obtain a lower plane of happiness and enjoyment and spend it with the other beings there, although he still feels happiness within and is not competitive. Or he might be more virtuous and have a greater mind, body and soul, and spend his eternity within a higher plane of interaction.

Eternity is real, earth is real but not lasting. It is a testing ground to eternity. The environmental setting of Heaven is better, yet part is similar to the environment of earth. There are also other distant areas that man will see which will be new to him.

In Heaven there is a constant, everlasting purity; it is not a place where wrong is done, it is a place where life is perfect. Man will have his desires fulfilled, as his desires then will be reasonable to God. Thus, a man on a higher plane may enjoy more beauty or physical pleasures than a man on a lower plane, although that was determined by that man on earth.

Hopefully, a man's relatives and friends will be in Heaven so that he may again enjoy their company, and they enjoy his. Even though one might be on a higher plane than another, there is the ability to visit another plane for a period of time. There are also times when all planes are brought together, then divided again.

One might desire to travel back, or into the future, in earthly reality of time. The appropriate pleasures of each being are fulfilled, whether they are as simple as dinner and dancing or as complex as God creating new environments and events. There are also times of praise and adoration of God, as well as personal friendships with him.

Time is never ending in Heaven and all days are one, and each is better that the last. Time is never ending and eternity is constant infinitely. Heaven is happiness; happiness is God.

Chapter XX

Fifteenth Book of Wisdom:

Self Reliance

Man must at times entrust his being to others throughout his life. Within the womb of his mother, at birth and as a child he must submit to and rely on his parents. Man must submit to the Chieftains, and rely on others' input of wisdom to help him make good decisions throughout life.

Yet man, above all, must rely on himself. He must strive to make his own decisions by his personal feelings. Man must use his personal intuition at every moment in life, whether he is hunting or at battle or contemplating marriage and family decisions. Man cannot solely rely on the Tribe, or the Chieftain's advice. God so desires that man not totally rely on Him, but man must exercise his own thought and will. Man, first of all, must be his own friend and advisor. Man must live with himself and his mind, his actions shall take place after he gains sufficient information and contemplates different ideas and the action concluding to the end result of thought.

Although Tribe and family are important and must be taken care of, each man is of greater importance to himself. Man must not be selfish, but think of himself first, before others, yet interdependently with others. Man must do what he believes is right in order to keep his mind content, and if he is virtuous, hopefully his actions are correct.

Man is to be himself, be what he is without any relevance or subjection to scrutiny of others, as long as his actions are moral and just.

Each man is responsible for the outcome of his family and the Tribe; yet, more importantly, he is responsible for himself and his soul as seen by the eyes of his Maker, God.

Man cannot rely solely or partially on good wishes or faith. Man must make his way and be self-sufficient. Man cannot rely on others. Man knows right from wrong and must act accordingly. Man must take charge of his own life and action, man is to be his own individual initiator and motivator toward perfection, as God so desires.

Chapter XXI

Sixteenth Book of Wisdom:

Duty

God created the universe and man for his pleasure. Therefore, it is man's duty to be just to God.

It is not only to maintain a pure society that man lives the life and Laws of Life, it is his duty. It is man's duty to God that he kill persons of evil; that animals and insects are not killed unnecessarily; that the environment is not raped or polluted; that peace is kept and wars unwanted; that we cherish our family and Tribe; that we are friends to God and also worship Him.

It is not only just that we do these things and more, but it is our duty.

In every thought and every action, man has a duty to:

- God

- Oneself

- Family

- Tribe

- Universe

God created man and the universe, and He sustains both; although the universe is subject to His will - man is subject to his own mind and will, and acts without force from God. It is our duty to act in a virtuous and moral manner throughout life; this brings pleasure to God. It is our duty to strive towards Heaven, not only for our own sake but, more importantly, for the pleasure it gives God.

Man's duty to his Creator is to make Him happy with man and nature. If the river is dammed up and it is to flow, man's duty is to fix it by undamming it. If men are evil in actions toward God and He is offended, it is man's duty to stop them. God will not force man on earth toward His desired will, it is up to the will of man. But, it is man's duty on earth to serve his Creator and make life pleasurable for God interdependently with all of His other creations.

Man's duty, above all, is to serve God on earth and in Heaven; when man acts for God, he acts in response to his virtue.

Man's duty is, above all else, to serve and please God. Man was created on earth to please God and that purpose must be kept. Our life is devoted to God, not for ourself, but for duty. God is the Master of the Universe and man has been proclaimed by God as Master of Earth. It is man's duty to keep the earth clean by ridding it of deviations leading to evil and all else that is displeasing to God; it is our duty to our Creator. He gave us this life of happiness and we must serve Him, not only because it is just, but, more importantly, because it is man's duty.

Chapter XXII

Seventeenth Book of Wisdom:

One With God

One

The mind, body and soul of man is to be the Temple of God. By living the life and the Laws of Life and living a virtuous life, this can, and must, be attained. When man lives such a life from birth until death, the spirit of God can live within his being. As man grows in holiness and devotion to God, the Spirit of God grows stronger and greater in man.

The Supreme Chief, Chief(s) and Chieftains of the Tribe possess the Spirit of God above all others. This is why they are the Chief(s), their decisions are not only wisely contemplated thoughts, but thoughts that are those of God. These persons are indwelled and overwhelmed to such a degree that, even though they are not God, they are a body, a near total intermittent percentage or consistent Temple of God. Thus, the pure Tribe is truly directed by the words that are God's.

One With God

Man may be one with the omnipotent God when he has a process of intention of thought and action that might be said to be like unto God.

This man has achieved such a high degree of perfection his mind and actions are then in time and harmony with all good creations of the earth, the sun, the moon, the water, the wind, the elements, and all else good from God. This man is so in tune with the universe that he is one with the universe, he is in harmony both on earth and in eternity.

Man is now a part of the true will of God and in this state he is one with God. His mind, speech and action become the subservient will of God. This is the desired state in life, to become a direct instrument of God to be able to be so indwelled by God that all actions are near perfection. All life has meaning and purpose, yet now man has attained such a level that God envelopes this man to such a degree that the man becomes a part and a reflection of God. This man is now cooperating with the omnipresence of God in man on earth. This man is now in the desired state of being, this man is the near perfect being. He has reached an ultimate goal of the Caddo, to attain near perfection and be pleasing to God.

About the Author

William Moss is a member of the Caddo Tribe of Oklahoma. He graduated in 1989 from the University of Oklahoma with a Bachelor of Arts Degree in History with a emphasis in American History and American Indian Studies, and has a secondary degree in Political Science. The author currently resides in Los Angeles, California.